WHERE WILL YOU FIND ME?

¿DÓNDE ME ENCONTRARÁS?

Grow a bilingual vocabulary by:

- **Looking** at pictures and words
- **Talking** about what you see
- **Touching** and naming objects
- **Using** questions to extend learning...
  Ask questions that invite children
  to share information.
  Begin your questions with words like...
  who, what, when, where and how.

Aumenta tu vocabulario bilingüe:

- **Mirando** las imágenes y las palabras
- **Hablando** de lo que ves
- **Tocando** y nombrando los objetos
- **Usando** preguntas para aumentar el aprendizaje...
  Usa preguntas que inviten a los niños a compartir
  la información.
  Empieza tus frases con el uso de estas palabras:
  ¿quién? ¿qué? ¿cuándo? ¿dónde? y ¿cómo?

These books support a series of educational games by Learning Props.
Estos libros refuerzan una serie de juegos educativos desarrollados por Learning Props.
Learning Props, L.L.C., P.O. Box 774, Racine, WI 53401-0774
1-877-776-7750   www.learningprops.com

Created by/**Creado por:** Bev Schumacher, Learning Props, L.L.C.
Graphic Design/**Diseñadora gráfica:** Bev Kirk
Images/**Fotos:** Hemera Technologies Inc., 123rf.com, Bev Kirk, Matthew 25 Ministries, Photos.com
Spanish Translation/**Traducción al español:** Myriam Sosa, Rosana Sartirana
Thanks to the Racine Zoological Society Conservation Education Department for technical support.
Gracias al Racine Zoological Society Conservation Education Department por el soporte técnico.

Library of Congress Control Number 2008907377   ISBN 978-1-935292-07-4

LEARNING *PROPS®*

 # At my home...
En mi casa...

pen and paper
la pluma y el papel

sink
el lavabo

dog
el perro

door
la puerta

mailbox
el buzón
del correo

flashlight
la linterna

key
la llave

shoes
los zapatos

lamp
la lámpara

couch
el sofá

phone
el teléfono

light switch
la llave de la luz

chair
el sillón

doorknob
el picaporte/
la perilla

bed
la cama

rug
el tapete/
la alfombra

flowers
las flores

 # In the kitchen...
En la cocina...

can opener
el abrelatas

oven mitt
el guante para
el horno/
la agarradera

measuring
spoons
las cucharas
para medir

refrigerator
el refrigerador/
la heladera

apple
la manzana

table and chair
la mesa y la silla

frying pan
la sartén

turner
la palita/
la espátula

mug
la taza

toaster
el tostador/
la tostadora

cookie
la galleta

place setting
la mesa puesta

pear
la pera

mixer
la batidora

banana
el plátano/
la banana

salt and pepper
shakers
el salero y
el pimentero

microwave
el horno
microondas

 # In the garage...
En el garaje...

ladder
la escalera

bike
la bicicleta

shovel
la pala

garden tools
las herramientas
de jardinería

hose
la manguera

paintbrush
la brocha

wheelbarrow
la carretilla

garbage can
el bote de
la basura

In the workshop...
En el taller...

nails
los clavos

hammer
el martillo

workbench
el banco
de trabajo

screws
los tornillos

drill
el taladro

saw
el serrucho

screwdrivers
los desarmadores/
los destornilladores

vise
el torno

clamp
la abrazadera

At school...
En la escuela...

students reading
los estudiantes leyendo

books
los libros

playground
el patio de juegos

puppets
los títeres

pencils
los lápices

computer
la computadora

clock
el reloj

jump rope
la cuerda para saltar/
la soga de saltar

scissors
las tijeras

blocks
los bloques

puzzle
el rompecabezas

xylophone
el xilófono/
el xilofón

chalkboard
el pizarrón

paper punch
la perforadora

chair
la silla

crayons
las crayolas/
los crayones

paints
las pinturas/
las témperas

At the park...
En el parque...

children playing
los niños jugando

people walking
la gente caminando

sparrow
el gorrión

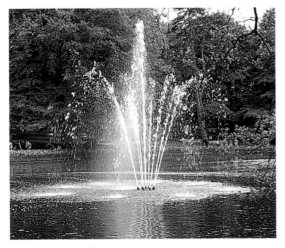

fountain
la fuente

geese
los gansos

playground
el patio de juegos

sailboat
el velero/
el barco de vela

pigeons
las palomas

tree
el árbol

fish
los peces

bench
la banca/el banco

In the city...
En la ciudad...

people
la gente

grocery store
el supermercado

escalator
**la escalera mecánica/
la escalera eléctrica**

buildings
los edificios

**traffic
light
el semáforo**

**umbrella
el paraguas**

**airplane
el avión**

**money
el dinero**

**signs
las señales**

**food
la comida**

**parking
meters
los parquímetros**

**car
el coche/el carro/el auto**

At the zoo...
En el zoológico...

elephant
el elefante

chimpanzees
los chimpancés

giraffe
la jirafa

peacock
el pavo real

zebras
las cebras

monkey
el mono/
el chango

flamingo
el flamenco/
el flamingo

tigers
los tigres

bear
el oso

 # At the farm...
En la granja...

cow
la vaca

apple tree
el manzanero/
el manzano

goats
las cabras

pigs
los cerdos/
los cochinos

sheep
la oveja

tractor
el tractor

crop
la cosecha/el cultivo

barn
el establo/el granero

horse
el caballo

chickens
las gallinas/los pollos

rooster
el gallo

hen
la gallina

ducks
los patos

At a party...
En una fiesta...

candles
las velitas

cake
**el pastel/
la torta**

balloons
los globos

gifts
los regalos

camera
la cámara

popcorn
**las palomitas
de maíz**

clown
el payaso

ribbons
los moños

cup
el vaso

card
la tarjeta

party hat
**el gorrito
de fiesta**

pronunciation la pronunciación

Where Will You Find Me?/**Wair Wil Yoo Finde Mee**?
  ¿Dónde Me Encontrarás?/¿**Dohn**-day May Ayn-kohn-trah-**rahs**?
  at my home/**at mye home** en mi casa/ayn mee **kah**-sah
  in the kitchen/**in** THuh **kich**-uhn en la cocina/ayn lah koh-**see**-nah
  in the garage/**in** THuh guh-**rahj** en el garaje/ayn ayl gah-**rah**-hay
  in the workshop/**in** THuh **wurk**-shop en el taller/ayn ayl tah-**yayr**
  at school/**at skool** en la escuela/ayn lah ays-koo-**ay**-lah
  at the park/**at** THuh **park** en el parque/ayn ayl **pahr**-kay
  in the city/**in** THuh **sit**-ee en la ciudad/ayn lah see-oo-**dahd**
  at the zoo/**at** THuh **zoo** en el zoológico/ayn ayl soh-**loh**-hee-koh
  at the farm/**at** THuh **farm** en la granja/ayn lah **grahn**-hah
  at a party/**at uh par**-tee en una fiesta/ayn **oo**-nah fee-**ays**-tah

airplane/**air**-plane el avión/ayl ah-vee-**ohn**
apple/**ap**-uhl la manzana/lah mahn-**sah**-nah
apple tree/**ap**-uhl **tree** el manzanero, el manzano/
ayl mahn-sah-**nay**-roh, ayl mahn-**sah**-noh
balloons/buh-**loonz** los globos/lohs **gloh**-bohs
banana/buh-**na**-nuh el plátano, la banana/
ayl **plah**-tah-noh, lah bah-**nah**-nah
barn/**barn** el establo, el granero/ayl ays-**tah**-bloh,
ayl grah-**nay**-roh
bear/**bair** el oso/ayl **oh**-soh
bed/**bed** la cama/lah **kah**-mah
bench/**bench** la banca, el banco/lah **bahn**-kah,
ayl **bahn**-koh
bike/**bike** la bicicleta/lah bee-see-**klay**-tah
blocks/**blokz** los bloques/lohs **bloh**-kays
books/**bukss** los libros/lohs **lee**-brohs
buildings/**bil**-dingz los edificios/
lohs ay-dee-**fee**-see-ohs
cake/**kayk** el pastel, la torta/ayl pahs-**tayl**, lah **tohr**-tah
camera/**kam**-ur-uh la cámara/lah **kah**-mah-rah
can opener/**kan oh**-puhn-ur el abrelatas/
ayl ah-bray-**lah**-tahs
candles/**kan**-duhlz las velitas/lahs vay-**lee**-tahs
car/**kar** el coche, el carro, el auto/ayl **koh**-shay,
ayl **kah**-rroh, ayl **ah**-oo-toh
card/**kard** la tarjeta/lah tahr-**hay**-tah
chair/**chair** el sillón, la silla/ayl see-**yohn**, la **see**-yah
chalkboard/**chawk**-bord el pizarrón/ayl pee-sah-**rrohn**
chickens/**chick**-uhnss las gallinas, los pollos/
lahs gah-**yee**-nahs, lohs **poh**-yohs
children playing/**chil**-drin **pla**-ying los niños jugando/
lohs **nee**-nyohs hoo-**gahn**-doh
chimpanzees/chim-**pan**-zeez los chimpancés/
lohs sheem-pahn-**says**
clamp/**klamp** la abrazadera/lah ah-brah-sah-**day**-rah

clock/**klok** el reloj/ayl ray-**lohgh**
clown/**kloun** el payaso/ayl pah-**yah**-soh
computer/kuhm-**pyoo**-tur la computadora/
lah kohm-poo-tah-**doh**-rah
cookie/**kuk**-ee la galleta/lah gah-**yay**-tah
couch/**kouch** el sofá/ayl soh-**fah**
cow/**kou** la vaca/lah **vah**-kah
crayons/**kray**-uhnz or **kray**-onz las crayolas,
los crayones/lahs krah-**yoh**-lahs, lohs krah-**yoh**-nays
crop/**krop** la cosecha, el cultivo/lah koh-**say**-shah,
ayl kool-**tee**-voh
cup/**kuhp** el vaso/ayl **vah**-soh
dog/**dawg** el perro/ayl **pay**-rroh
door/**dor** la puerta/lah poo-**ayr**-tah
doorknob/**dor**-nob el picaporte, la perilla/
ayl pee-kah-**pohr**-tay, lah pay-**ree**-yah
drill/**dril** el taladro/ayl tah-**lah**-droh
ducks/**duhkz** los patos/lohs **pah**-tohs
elephant /**el**-uh-fuhnt el elefante/ayl ay-lay-**fahn**-tay
escalator/**ess**-kuh-lay-tur la escalera mecánica,
la escalera eléctrica/lah ays-kah-**lay**-rah may-**kah**-nee-kah,
lah ays-kah-**lay**-rah ay-**layk**-tree-kah
fish/**fish** los peces/lohs **pay**-says
flamingo/fluh-**ming**-goh el flamenco, el flamingo/
ayl flah-**mayn**-koh, ayl flah-**meen**-goh
flashlight/**flash**-lite la linterna/lah leen-**tayr**-nah
flowers/**flou**-urz las flores/lahs **floh**-rays
food /**food** la comida/lah koh-**mee**-dah
fountain/**foun**-tuhn la fuente/lah foo-**ayn**-tay
frying pan/**frye**-ing **pan** la sartén/lah sahr-**tayn**
garbage can/**gar**-bij **kan** el bote de la basura/
ayl **boh**-tay day lah bah-**soo**-rah
garden tools/**gard**-uhn **toolz** las herramientas de
jardinería/lahs ay-rrah-mee-**ayn**-tahs day
hahr-dee-nay-**ree**-ah

geese/**geess** los gansos/lohs **gahn**-sohs
gifts/**giftss** los regalos/lohs rray-**gah**-lohs
giraffe/juh-**raf** la jirafa/lah hee-**rah**-fah
goats/**gohtss** las cabras/lahs **kah**-brahs
grocery store/**groh**-sur-ree **stor** el supermercado/
ayl soo-payr-mayr-**kah**-doh
hammer/**ham**-ur el martillo/ayl mahr-**tee**-yoh
hen/**hen** la gallina/lah gah-**yee**-nah
horse/**horss** el caballo/ayl kah-**bah**-yoh
hose/**hohz** la manguera/lah mahn-**gay**-rah
jump rope/**juhmp rohp** la cuerda para saltar, la soga de
saltar/lah koo-**ayr**-dah **pah**-rah sahl-**tahr**, lah **soh**-gah
day sahl-**tahr**
key/**kee** la llave/lah **yah**-vay
ladder/**lad**-ur la escalera/lah ays-kah-**lay**-rah
lamp/**lamp** la lámpara/lah **lahm**-pah-rah
light switch/**lite swich** la llave de la luz/lah **yah**-vay day
lah loos
mailbox/**mayl**-boks el buzón del correo/ayl boo-**sohn**
dayl koh-**rray**-oh
measuring spoons/**mezh**-ur-ing **spoonz** las cucharas
para medir/lahs koo-**shah**-rahs **pah**-rah may-**deer**
microwave/**mye**-kroh-wave el horno microondas/
ayl **ohr**-noh mee-kroh-**ohn**-dahs
mixer/**miks**-ur la batidora/lah bah-tee-**doh**-rah
money/**muhn**-ee el dinero/ayl dee-**nay**-roh
monkey/**muhng**-kee el mono, el chango/ayl **moh**-noh,
ayl **shahn**-goh
mug/**muhg** la taza/lah **tah**-sah
nails/**naylz** los clavos/lohs **klah**-vohs
oven mitt/**uhv**-uhn **mit** el guante para el horno,
la agarradera/ayl goo-**ahn**-tay **pah**-rah ayl **ohr**-noh,
lah ah-gah-rrah-**day**-rah
paintbrush/**paynt**-bruhsh la brocha/lah **broh**-sha
paints/**payntss** las pinturas, las témperas/
lahs peen-**too**-rahs, lahs **taym**-pay-rahs
paper punch/**pay**-pur **puhnch** la perforadora/
lah payr-foh-rah-**doh**-rah
parking meters/**par**-king **mee**-turz los parquímetros/
lohs pahr-**kee**-may-trohs
party hat/**par**-tee **hat** el gorrito de fiesta/
ayl goh-**rree**-toh day fee-**ays**-tah
peacock/**pee**-kok el pavo real/ayl **pah**-voh rray-**ahl**
pear/**pair** la pera/lah **pay**-rah
pen and paper/**pen and pay**-pur la pluma y el papel/
lah **ploo**-mah ee ayl pah-**payl**
pencils/**pen**-suhlz los lápices/lohs **lah**-pee-says
people/**pee**-puhl la gente/lah **hayn**-tay
people walking/**pee**-puhl **waw**-king la gente caminando/
lah **hayn**-tay kah-mee-**nahn**-doh
phone/**fohn** el teléfono/ayl tay-**lay**-foh-noh
pigeons/**pij**-uhnz las palomas/lahs pah-**loh**-mahs
pigs/**pigz** los cerdos, los cochinos/lohs **sayr**-dohs,
lohs koh-**shee**-nohs

place setting/**playss set**-ting la mesa puesta/
lah **may**-sah poo-**ays**-tah
playground/**play**-ground el patio de juegos/
ayl **pah**-tee-oh day hoo-**ay**-gohs
popcorn/**pop**-korn las palomitas de maíz/
lahs pah-loh-**mee**-tahs day mah-**ees**
puppets/**puhp**-itss los títeres/lohs **tee**-tay-rays
puzzle/**puhz**-uhl el rompecabezas/
ayl rrohm-pay-kah-**bay**-sahs
refrigerator/ri-**frij**-uh-ray-tur el refrigerador, la heladera/
ayl rray-free-hay-rah-**dohr**, lah ay-lah-**day**-rah
ribbons/**rib**-uhnz los moños/lohs **moh**-nyohs
rooster/**roo**-stur el gallo/ayl **gah**-yoh
rug/**ruhg** el tapete, la alfombra/ayl tah-**pay**-tay,
lah ahl-**fohm**-brah
sailboat/**sayl**-boht el velero, el barco de vela/
ayl vay-**lay**-roh, ayl **bahr**-koh day **vay**-lah
salt and pepper shakers/**sawlt and pep**-ur **shayk**-urz
el salero y el pimentero/ayl sah-**lay**-roh ee ayl
pee-mahn-**tay**-roh
saw/**saw** el serrucho/ayl say-**rroo**-shoh
scissors/**siz**-urz las tijeras/lahs tee-**hay**-rahs
screwdrivers/**skroo**-drye-vurz los desarmadores,
los destornilladores/lohs days-ahr-mah-**doh**-rays,
lohs days-tohr-nee-yah-**doh**-rays
screws/**skrooz** los tornillos/lohs tohr-**nee**-yohs
sheep/**sheep** la oveja/lah oh-**vay**-hah
shoes/**shooz** los zapatos/lohs sah-**pah**-tohs
shovel/**shuhv**-uhl la pala/lah **pah**-lah
signs/**sinez** las señales/lahs say-**nyah**-lays
sink/**singk** el lavabo/ayl lah-**vah**-boh
sparrow/**spa**-roh el gorrión/ayl goh-rree-**ohn**
students reading/ **stood**-uhntss **ree**-ding
los estudiantes leyendo/lohs ays-too-dee-**ahn**-tays
lay-**yayn**-doh
table and chair/**tay**-buhl **and chair** la mesa y la silla/
lah **may**-sah ee lah **see**-yah
tigers/**tye**-gurz los tigres/lohs **tee**-grays
toaster/**tohss**-tur el tostador, la tostadora/
ayl tohs-tah-**dohr**, lah tohs-tah-**doh**-rah
tractor/**trak**-tur el tractor/ayl trahk-**tohr**
traffic light/**traf**-ik **lite** el semáforo/ayl say-**mah**-foh-roh
tree/**tree** el árbol/ayl **ahr**-bohl
turner/**turn**-ur la palita, la espátula/lah pah-**lee**-tah,
lah ays-**pah**-too-lah
umbrella/uhm-**brel**-uh el paraguas/ayl pah-**rah**-goo-ahs
vise/**visse** el torno/ayl **tohr**-noh
wheelbarrow/**weel**-ba-roh la carretilla/
lah kah-rray-**tee**-yah
workbench/**wurk**-bench el banco de trabajo/
ayl **bahn**-koh day trah-**bah**-hoh
xylophone/**zye**-luh-fone el xilófono, el xilofón/
ayl xee-**loh**-pho-noh, ayl xee-loh-**fohn**
zebras/**zee**-bruhz las cebras/lahs **say**-brahs